D1243637

CATS

Jolyon Goddard

Grolier
an imprint of

www.scholastic.com/librarypublishing

Published 2009 by Grolier
An Imprint of Scholastic Library Publishing
Old Sherman Turnpike
Danbury, Connecticut 06816

For The Brown Reference Group plc
Project Editor: Jolyon Goddard
Picture Researcher: Clare Newman
Designer: Sarah Williams
Managing Editor: Tim Harris

Volume ISBN-13: 978-0-7172-8038-4
Volume ISBN-10: 0-7172-8038-1

Library of Congress Cataloging-in-Publication Data

Nature's children. Set 5.
p. cm.
Includes index.
ISBN-13: 978-0-7172-8084-1
ISBN-10: 0-7172-8084-5 (set)
1. Animals--Encyclopedias, Juvenile. I. Grolier (Firm)
QL49.N386 2009
590.3--dc22
2008014674

Printed and bound in China

PICTURE CREDITS

Front Cover: **Shutterstock**: Petra Wegner.

Back Cover: **Shutterstock**: Gregor Kervina, Christophe Rolland, Gina Smith, Krissy Van Alstyne.

Corbis: Roger Wood 9; **NaturePL**: Jane Burton 33, 42; **Photolibrary**: Juniors Bildarchiv 34; **Shutterstock**: Annette 41, Tony Campbell 10, Cindy Lynn Dockrill 2–3, Anna Dzondzua 6, Massimo Fiorentini 29, Babusi Octavian Florentin 13, Eric Isselee 4, Sebastian Knight 21, Debbie Oetgen 45, Alin Popescu 17, Tina Rencelj 38, Rgbspace 22, Magdalena Szachowska 18, Denis Tabler 37, Trutta55 14, Suzanne Tucker 26–27, Anna Utekhina 5, 46, Zhorov Igor Vladimirovich 30.

Contents

FACT FILE: Cats

Class	Mammals (Mammalia)
Order	Carnivores (Carnivora)
Family	Cat family (Felidae)
Genus	Wildcats, domestic, or pet, cats, and various other small cats (*Felis*)
Species	Wildcats and domestic cats (*Felis silvestris*)
Subspecies	Domestic cats (*Felis silvestris catus*)
World distribution	Cats are kept as pets worldwide; wildcats still live in Europe, Asia, and Africa
Habitat	Pet cats often live indoors; many are allowed to roam outside; wildcats live in many habitats, including deserts, grasslands, and woodlands
Distinctive physical characteristics	Agile, flexible body good at running, jumping, and climbing; eyes reflect light; long whiskers on face; pointed ears; short or long hair
Habits	Hunt for food; more active at night; spend a lot of time grooming themselves; usually solitary
Diet	Pet cats eat meat-based cat food; outdoors, cats will catch and eat rodents, birds, fish, lizards, and some insects

Introduction

There are many reasons why cats are among the most popular pets in the world. They are graceful, athletic animals with adorable faces and large, beautiful eyes. Cats are independent, and yet enjoy giving and receiving affection. They make an endearing **purr** when stroked—a sound that is relaxing for both the owner and pet.

Cats come in an amazing variety of coat colors, from white, gray, and smoky blue to ginger, rich brown, or black—or a mixture of colors. All of these reasons and more make cats the "purr-fect" pet for many people.

With proper care, these kittens will live to at least 15 years old.

Tabby markings are a pattern of stripes, blotches, or spots. They are common in pet cats and are shared by wildcats. This coloration helps the cats blend into their surroundings when they hunt.

Natural Hunters

There are 37 **species**, or types, of cats, broadly split in two groups: big cats and small cats. Big cats include lions, tigers, cheetahs, jaguars, and leopards. Small cats are a much larger group and include cougars, lynx, servals, ocelots, **domestic** cats, and many more species of cats.

All cats are hunters, supremely equipped with sharp claws and stabbing and cutting teeth. Cats are born with a strong desire, or instinct, to hunt. The jumping and pouncing games that **kittens** play are practice for when the animals will have to find their own food as adults. Indoor cats will never get the chance to hunt mice, rats, birds, or fish. However, no matter how well fed or pampered a cat is, it still has the hunting instinct of its wildcat **ancestors**.

History Lesson

Cats have lived with or around humans for at least 8,000 years. When humans first started to grow crops, they had a problem with **rodents**, such as rats and mice. These pests would nibble away at stored grains and other foods. In turn, the rats and mice attracted wildcats. People realized that the cats were being very helpful by killing and eating the pesky rodents. Soon, cats were living as domestic animals with people.

No one knows exactly who first domesticated wildcats, but all domestic cats are descended from African wildcats. These wildcats are found naturally in northern Africa and western Asia. The ancient Egyptians particularly liked cats—they even worshiped a cat-headed goddess called Bastet.

Since they were first tamed, domestic cats have developed differences from their wildcat ancestors. Domestic cats have many different fur colors, whereas wildcats are **tabbies**. Domestic cats are smaller. They also keep some kittenlike characteristics, such as playfulness, as adults.

In ancient Egypt, cat owners would shave off their eyebrows as a sign of grief when their cat died. The punishment for killing a cat was death!

A young farm cat spots prey. Cats hunt more than 1,000 different species of animals for food.

Mousers

In ancient times, domestic cats were highly sought after for their pest-control skills. They began to spread from northern Africa. By 3,000 years ago, **mousers** were common across Europe. They then spread across Asia, as far as Japan. It also became common for ships to have cats. These mousers kept down the numbers of rodents gnawing away at the ships' food stores. The cats would often "escape" onto dry land when the ship docked. By the 1700s, ships' cats had spread to North and South America, and in the 1800s they reached Australia.

To this day, cats are still often used as working animals. They keep down the numbers of mice and rats on farms and ships, in stores, and even in homes. Some cats will play with their prey before killing it. They often bring the animals they have caught to their owner. Some experts think that cats do that because they see their owner as a poor hunter that cannot catch his or her own food!

Agile Animals

The **feline** body is built for speed. A cat's muscular legs allow it to run at 30 miles (48 km) per hour in short bursts. Cats can also leap up to five times their height.

Cats have more bones in their spine than human's do. That gives them greater flexibility. They can twist and turn in midair when jumping or chasing a bird.

Cats also have amazing balance and do not seem bothered by heights. Walking along the top of a fence, a thin ledge, or a branch high in a tree poses no problem whatsoever. The long tail acts as a counterbalance as a cat moves. If the cat does fall, it uses its sense of balance to twist itself around midair. That way it lands on its feet without injury. This ability to land safely is known as the "righting reflex."

Like a tightrope walker, a cat tiptoes with perfect balance along a fence.

In daylight, the pupils of a domestic cat's eyes narrow to a vertical slit.

Super Senses

Cats have amazing senses. When hunting in the dark, a cat relies on its highly developed eyesight. A reflective layer at the back of the eye helps the cat make the most of dim light at night, when it is most active. Its **pupils** open wide to let in as much light as possible. Cats do have some color vision, but it is much poorer than a human's.

A cat's hearing is very sharp. They can easily detect the high-pitched squeaks of rodents. Cats can turn their ears separately to pinpoint the source of a sound. Cats use smell to hunt, too. Like many mammals, they have a **Jacobson's organ** in their mouth. This organ "tastes" chemicals in the air, especially the scent of other cats. Their sense of taste is well developed, too.

The sensory whiskers on a cat's face help the animal judge space around itself in darkness. If the whiskers—which are wider than the width of the cat—can fit through a space untouched, so can the rest of the cat. Whiskers also detect air movements around objects, giving the cat radarlike information about its surroundings.

In and Out

Some pet cats, such as those that live in city apartments, spend their whole life indoors. These cats tend to be more affectionate with people. They can get bored, so they need toys and a lot of companionship. Housebound cats tend to live longer, because they are at less risk of being hit by a car or catching diseases from other cats. However, they face a greater risk of becoming overweight due to less exercise.

Cats that can move from the indoors to the outdoors as they please have a much more natural existence than housebound cats. They can roam, hunt, interact with other cats, and get plenty of exercise. However, they face many risks. These include fighting with other cats, being attacked by dogs, catching diseases from other cats, getting lost, and being hit by cars. These cats are often more independent and less affectionate than housebound cats.

Cats, such as this Siamese, that are used to roaming outside can get frustrated if kept indoors. They will sit by a window, on the lookout for other cats or prey.

The Abyssinian cat resembles the cats seen in ancient Egyptian carvings and paintings. It is a quiet breed, but very playful and curious.

Different Breeds

There are many kinds, or **breeds**, of domestic cats. Different breeds have their own unique body and face shape, type of coat, and, sometimes, personality. Breeds develop when cats are isolated in a part of the world, and certain physical characteristics begin to dominate. Today, however, breeds are more likely to come about by people mixing together existing breeds to create new cats with unique features. There are more than 100 breeds and varieties of cats, and new ones are being developed all the time. Some recent breeds are a mixture of domestic cats and other small cats. For example, the Bengal is part Asian leopard cat.

Breeds are divided into shorthairs and longhairs. Well-known shorthairs include the Siamese, Burmese, tailless Manx, Abyssinian, and curly-haired Cornish Rex. There are even some bald-looking cats, such as the Sphynx. These cats actually have a layer of downy hair, but it is usually only visible at close range. Long-haired cats include the Persian, Maine coon, Norwegian forest cat, and Turkish Van.

All Mixed Up

Most pet cats, farm cats, and domestic cats that live wild are not purebreds. They are mongrels, or mutts—a mixture of breeds. They come in different body shapes and sizes. Their coat may be one color, two colors, **tortoiseshell**, or tabby. Tortoiseshell is a mixture of red and black fur. Tortoiseshell-and-white coloration is called **calico**. Mongrels may have thick or thin hair, depending on their ancestors. They are usually shorthairs. Many mongrels have a compact body shape, known as "cobby."

Cats have four types of hairs. Short crimped down hairs form an undercoat that traps and warms air against the body. Slightly longer awn hairs make up a middle coat. This coat protects the down hairs and helps keep the cat warm, too. The longer guard hairs form an outer coat that protects the cat against wind and rain. The longest hairs are the sensory **vibrissae**, which include the whiskers on the cat's face.

Mixed-bred cats often have an interesting mixture of coat colors, such as this tortoiseshell and white.

To pick up a cat, place one hand under its front legs, and with the other hand, scoop up its backside. Never lift a cat by grabbing it around the middle, lifting it by its tail, or picking it up by the or scruff of its neck.

Choosing a Pet

Owning a cat is a big commitment. Before getting a pet cat, you must make sure that you will be able to give it a good home, afford to keep it, feed it at regular times, and spend plenty of time with it. It is often best to get two cats, so that they can keep each other company if no one else is around.

Some people pay a lot of money for a purebred kitten—sometimes thousands of dollars. Others find a pet from a shelter, or animal sanctuary, such as the one run by the American Society for the Prevention of Cruelty to Animals (ASPCA).

The cats in shelters are usually **neutered** and **vaccinated** against serious diseases. Shelters have many cats. There are almost always kittens if you want a younger, more playful cat. If you want a less boisterous pet, an older cat is a better choice. Cats have different personalities—some will want a lot of attention, whereas others will be more independent. Make sure the cat you get is healthy. It should be active with bright, clear eyes, a glossy coat, and clean ears.

Settling In

The first few days in a new home can be a very scary time for a cat. That is especially true, if the cat is a kitten. Finding itself alone in a strange place is very unnerving to a young kitten, when it is used to curling up against its mother with its siblings.

To help a cat settle in comfortably, it should be kept in a warm room for its first few days. If it is a kitten, place a hot-water bottle wrapped in a towel in its bed. The warmth will remind the kitten of its mother's body. In addition, a ticking clock in the room will remind the kitten of its mother's heartbeat.

Make sure the cat has a cozy bed. It will also need plenty of toys. Food and water bowls and a litter box should be placed in a corner of the room away from the cat's bed. Do not handle the cat too much in these early days. When the cat is comfortable with you and your family, introduce it to other household pets one by one. The cat will also need an identification tag on a collar if it is going to be allowed outdoors.

Favorite Foods

Cats are meat eaters, or carnivores. They do eat some plant foods occasionally, too. Commercial cat food contains meat, such as fish or chicken, and added nutrients, such as calcium. Try to vary the flavors of cat food. Otherwise, your cat may become very picky. It may get used to just one kind of food and refuse other brands or flavors offered to it. Be sure to never give pet dog food to a cat—it contains substances that are poisonous to cats.

Cats also need water. However, they will not drink from a bowl if they can taste detergent. That sometimes happens if a bowl hasn't been rinsed thoroughly. A cat will find puddles or ponds to drink from instead. Bowls for water and food should, therefore, be rinsed thoroughly after being washed. Do not give cats cow's milk because it is not healthy for them.

Persians are one of the most popular long-haired breeds of cats. They have a short nose, which often leads to breathing difficulties.

Keeping Clean

Cats are very clean animals. They groom their fur several times each day, especially after eating. Grooming keeps a cat's fur and skin healthy. A matted, dirty coat doesn't keep a cat warm.

A cat's tongue is covered in tiny backward-pointing hooks. These hooks make the tongue rough—which is ideal not only for brushing fur but also for rasping meat off the bones of prey animals. A cat uses its front teeth to remove tangles in its fur. It also licks its paws and uses them to groom parts of its body the tongue cannot reach, such as the sides of the head.

Pet cats love being stroked and brushed by their owners. Longhairs need brushing once a day to keep their fur tangle-free. That also prevents them from swallowing too many of the tangled knots they remove when grooming themselves. (Cats often cough up the swallowed hair in the form of "fur balls.") Pet cats really love to be stroked or rubbed in hard-to-reach places, such as behind the ears.

A cat's saliva acts as a deodorant. Without a strong odor, a cat is protected from enemies that hunt by smell.

Cats sleep for 12 to 16 hours each day. That includes many short snoozes or "cat naps."

Purring Pussycats

For many cat owners, a cat's purr is one of their favorite sounds. Most people associate purring with contentment. However, cats purr in other situations, too. Cats that are in pain, frightened, or are dying will purr. Cats first learn to purr at about one week old. It is a sign to the mother cat that her kittens are fine and getting enough milk. No one knows exactly how cats purr, but some experts think that it is similar to humans snoring!

Cats make many other noises to communicate with other cats, their enemies, and their human owners. Cats meow to their human owners as a greeting, when they want food, when they want to go outside, or when they are not happy. Fighting and **mating** cats screech, wail, howl, growl, hiss, snarl, and spit. Cats use body language to communicate, too. They wag their tail when agitated. They flatten their ears and crouch low when threatened by another cat. They arch their back and bristle their fur to make themselves look bigger to dogs and other enemies.

Catnip

Catnip is part of the mint family. This leafy herb contains an oil that has a strange effect on some—but not all—cats. When a cat finds a catnip plant, it will chew its leaves or roll around in it purring, meowing, or even growling. Some cats react more energetically and become very playful. They may race around before falling asleep, often in an unusual position. The effects of catnip last about 15 minutes. It is totally harmless.

Many cat owners grow catnip outdoors. Toys stuffed with catnip are also available. Cats usually first develop a taste for catnip at about three months of age—kittens younger than that show no interest in the herb. Other plants, such as valerian and honeysuckle, have a similar affect as catnip on some cats.

About half of all adult cats react to the effects of catnip.

If carefully trained, kittens can learn to use a litter box from an early age.

House-training

Pet cats are much easier to housebreak than pet dogs. They happily use a litter box to relieve themselves once they've learned what it is for. However, cats are much more difficult to train to obey commands, such as, "SIT," "STAY," or "COME." Also, it's not in a cat's nature to be walked on a leash. They are much too independent to be told what to do!

Cats do have some bad habits, such as scratching furniture with their claws. They do that to remove the outer layer so their claws stay sharp. They also scratch furniture to scent mark their **territory**. An indoor cat will see its home as its territory. Buying a scratching post may stop a cat from scratching furniture. Outdoor cats have a territory, too. They scent mark their territory with scratch marks, urine, and droppings. Many cats bury their droppings in soil, but males, especially those that have not been neutered, do not. Cats will scent mark people, too—by rubbing the sides of their head against a person's legs or hands!

Healthy Cats

Cats that are well cared for are usually healthy and free of disease. However, from time to time a cat will get ill. Common signs of illness are sleepiness, loss of appetite, a runny nose, vomiting, and diarrhea. Some cats will drink more water than usual when sick. A dirty, matted coat is also a sign that a cat is ill. Most cat illnesses are short-lived and the cat recovers within a day or two. However, if the illness persists, the cat should be examined and, if necessary, treated by a veterinarian, or vet.

Vets can give cats shots, or vaccinations, to prevent serious diseases, such rabies, cat flu, and feline leukemia. They might also give medicine to treat **parasites**, such as worms, ticks, fleas, and ear mites. In addition, vets can neuter cats, which prevents them from reproducing. Once neutered, a cat is much less territorial. It will no longer spray its smelly urine to mark its territory.

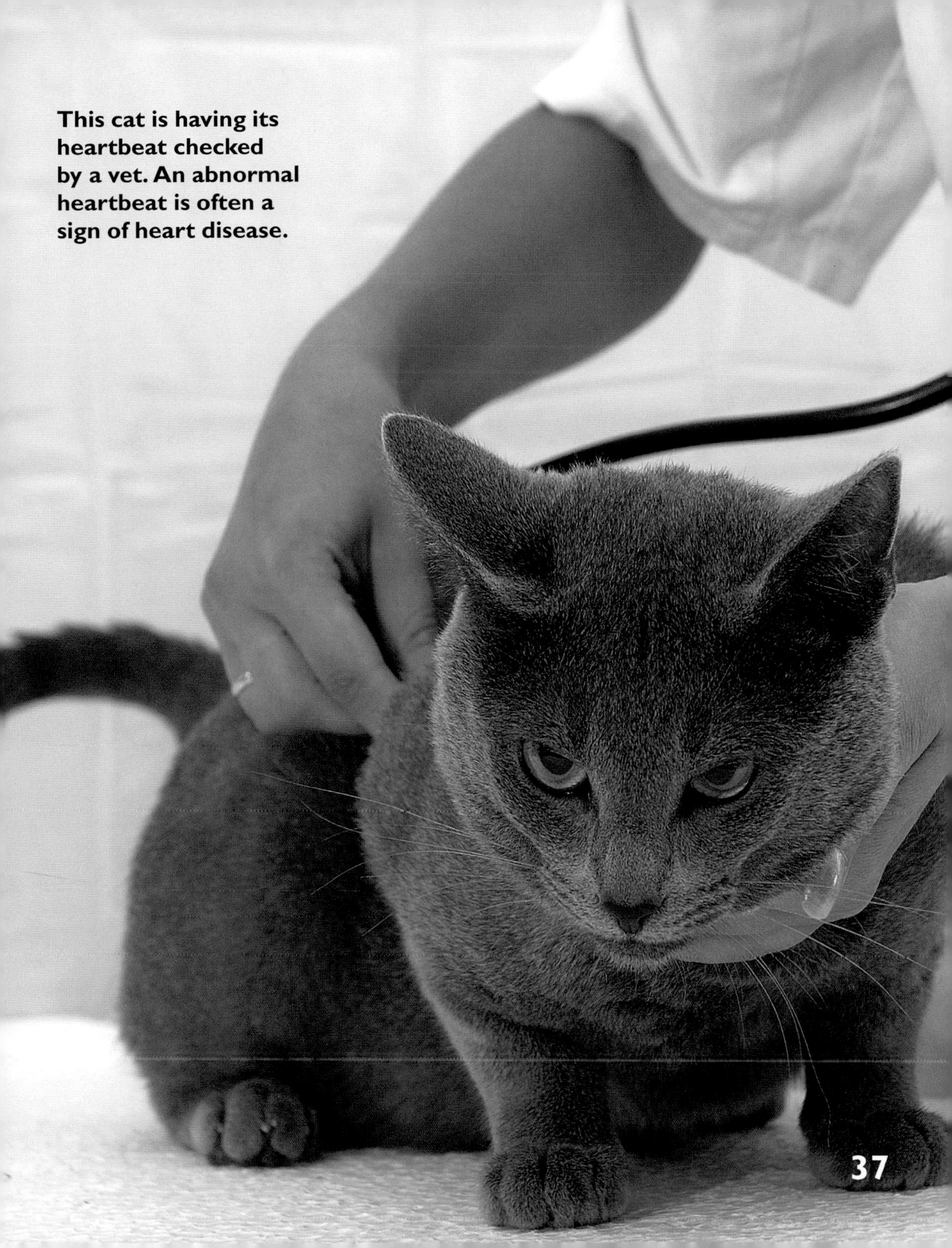

This cat is having its heartbeat checked by a vet. An abnormal heartbeat is often a sign of heart disease.

A labrador retriever dog and a young ginger tabby snuggle up.

Pet Pals

Although many cats are loners, some prefer to live with other cats or even dogs! If two or more cats live together, there will be some fighting until a hierarchy, from the "top cat" to the "bottom cat" is established. Once this social structure is in place, however, cats sharing a home can become friends. They often snuggle up to and groom one another.

Cats and dogs are famous for not getting along. A cat will usually run away from a dog. However, if a cat stands its ground, snarling, hissing, and arching its back to look bigger, a dog will usually back away. It knows that the cat's sharp claws can do a lot of damage. If a cat and dog are introduced to each other when both are young, they are much more likely to get along. The cat is generally the dominant partner, or boss, in the friendship. They may still fight, especially when the dog wants to play—since a dog's idea of play usually involves nuzzling and licking the not-so-playful cat!

Noisy Courtship

Adult female cats that have not been neutered are called queens. They are ready to mate, or are "in heat," two or three times each year. During this time, the female calls to males, or tom cats, at night. She gives off a scent that usually attracts several males. The toms fight among themselves over which one gets to mate with the female.

However, in the end, the female decides which male can mate with her. It is usually the tom that owns the territory she is in. But even when the "chosen" tom approaches, the female may still lash out.

A female may be in heat for several days and might mate with several toms in that time.

Tom cats make a lot of noise—called caterwauling—when fighting other toms.

Newborn kittens drink milk from their mother.

Kitten Season

A queen is pregnant for about nine weeks. When she is ready to give birth, she finds a cozy place, where she will not be disturbed. Cats usually give birth in late spring and early summer, when the weather is warmer. They generally give birth at night and produce a **litter** of up to eight kittens. Each kitten is born wrapped in a thin film called a birth sac. The mother helps the kitten out of the sac and licks the youngster's face. The licking clears the kitten's mouth and nostrils of mucus so it can breathe properly.

A kitten cannot see when it is born—its eyes are sealed shut. It is also deaf. It has strong senses of smell and touch, which help it locate its mother's rich milk. If your cat has kittens, it is best to leave them alone and not touch them at this critical time when the mother is bonding with her young.

Playtime

Kittens' eyes open seven to ten days after birth. By two weeks, they can be handled for short periods of time. That way they will become used to being picked up and stroked. The young animals grow fast. By four weeks, they are ready to explore their surroundings, and they begin to play with their siblings. Young kittens also like to pounce on their mother's tail. Their play-fighting is good practice for when they will hunt. They learn to creep up silently on one another and pounce. That type of play is good practice for catching mice. They learn to jump up and catch insects in their paws, which is good practice for catching birds. They also learn to scoop up objects from the floor. That technique will help them catch fish.

After six weeks, kittens can start being **weaned**. They eat solid food, such as special kitten food, in addition to drinking their mother's milk. From eight weeks, kittens are old enough to go to new homes. Kittens reach adulthood at about six months. If given plenty of affection and good care, they can live to at least 15 years old or more.

All kittens are born with blue eyes. They rarely stay blue, however. At about three months they begin to change color. Feline eye colors include yellow, orange, green, and brown.

The Cornish rex was first bred in the 1950s in the United Kingdom. It does not have guard hairs, just curly awn and down hairs.

Showtime

People with purebred cats sometimes take them to cat shows to see if they can win prizes for being perfect examples of their breeds. Showing cats is known as "cat fancy," and it is very popular.

The Cat Fanciers' Association (CFA) is the largest cat club in the United States. It was set up in 1906 and now sponsors hundreds of shows each year. The CFA recognizes about 40 breeds of cats. But this number is bound to increase as new breeds of cats are developed.

Cat shows are a great place for people to see different breeds, from familiar Siamese, American shorthairs, and Persians to exotic Japanese bobtails, Ocicats, and Egyptian maus. Most shows also have a prize for the best household cat, or mongrel.

Feral Felines

Some cats return to live and breed in the wild. They are called **feral**. Some live alone, others form loose groups, often in and around farms. In cities, feral cats often live in big groups called colonies. These colonies are made up of smaller groups of closely related female cats and their kittens. The kittens in these groups often nurse from more than one queen. Feral tom cats live alone or in small groups.

Cats that are born feral are not tame. Those in towns and cities will approach humans for food, but they do not like to be petted. Feral cats in the countryside have a harder life. They are at risk from being attacked by big **predators**, such as coyotes. In many countries, special organizations trap feral cats. They neuter and vaccinate the cats and treat them for parasites before releasing them. Feral kittens are often taken in by cat shelters, where they can be adopted as pets. Feral cats make challenging pets. But with patience and gentle care, they usually get used to people and become rewarding and affectionate pets.

Words to Know

Ancestors	The early types of an existing animal.
Breeds	Kinds of domestic cats, such as Siamese and Persian.
Calico	A cat with a tortoiseshell (black and red) and white coat.
Domestic	Raised and bred by humans.
Feline	Describing cats; a cat.
Feral	When a domestic animal returns to the wild to live and breed.
Jacobson's organ	A sensory structure in a cat's mouth that "tastes" scents in the air.
Kittens	Young domestic cats.
Litter	A group of young born to the same mother at the same time.
Mating	Coming together to produce young.
Mousers	Cats that help humans by catching rats and mice.
Neutered	Given an operation to prevent an animal from having young.

Parasites	Animals that live on or in other animals, feeding on their skin, blood, and other body tissues.
Predators	Animals that hunt other animals.
Pupils	The dark openings at the front of eyes. Pupils expand in dim light.
Purr	A rhythmic vibrating sound made by a cat when content, frightened, or injured.
Rodents	Small mammals with gnawing teeth. Mice and rats are types of rodents.
Species	The scientific word for animals of the same kind that breed together.
Tabbies	Cats with a striped, blotched, or spotty coat.
Territory	An area an animal defends as its own private space.
Tortoiseshell	A black and red coat.
Vaccinated	Given medicines, often as injections, that prevent certain diseases.
Vibrissae	Sensory hairs such as whiskers.
Weaned	When a young mammal's diet changes from milk to adult food.

Find Out More

Books

Cat. Eyewitness Books. New York: DK Publishing, Inc., 2004.

Crisp, M. *Everything Cat: What Kids Really Want to Know About Cats*. Kids' FAQs. Minnetonka, Minnesota: NorthWord Books for Young Readers, 2003.

Web sites

For Kids… About Cats
kids.cfa.org/
Feline education for youngsters from the Cat Fanciers' Association.

Pet Care: Cat Care
www.aspca.org/site/PageServer?pagename=pets_catcare
Read expert advice from the American Society for the Prevention of Cruelty to Animals (ASPCA) on cat care.

Index